Duets for Dog Lovers

Early Elementary Duets for 1 Piano, 4 Paws

Margaret Goldston

FOREWORD

In this collection of duets the primo and secondo parts are EQUAL IN DIFFICULTY. Hand positions for the beginning of each piece are shown; however, easy position changes occur within some of the pieces.

Teachers and students alike will be richly rewarded with the benefits derived from duets. Practicing piano can be a lonely experience, but the "work" becomes "play" when sharing it with someone else. Duets help pupils learn to keep a steady rhythm and achieve continuity in performance. Also, duets add variety to the lesson plan or recital program. Teachers of group lessons use duets as an indispensable part of their class activities.

In addition to group classes, the two parts can be assigned to a sister and brother, child and parent, neighbors, or students with lessons scheduled consecutively without arranging extra practices. I made the discovery that many parents of my students had in the past studied piano sufficiently to be able to play the easy second part. The shared family activity resulted in increased parental interest and support.

My students who tried the duets were in the first level of their piano method. Contributing to our success was the fact that we combined the parts only AFTER mastering them separately and then with a very slow tempo and counting aloud. So enthusiastic were the students about *Duets for Dog Lovers* that I had a delightful time teaching them! I hope you have a similar experience.

CONTENTS

© Copyright MCMLXXXIX by Alfred Publishing Co., Inc.

The Bow-Wow Chorus

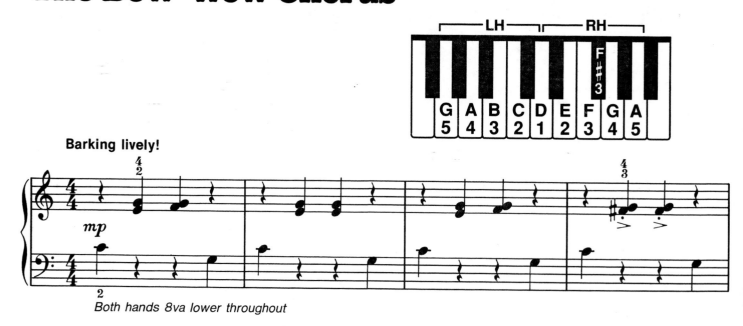

Barking lively!

Both hands 8va lower throughout

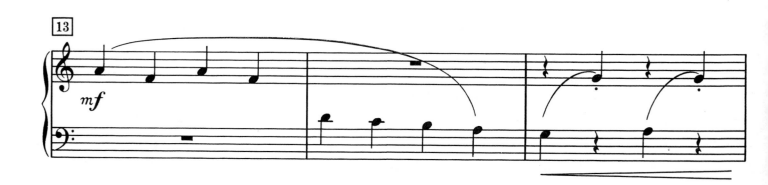

The Bow-Wow Chorus

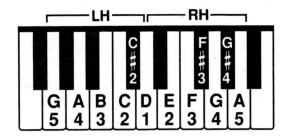

Barking lively!

Both hands 8va higher throughout

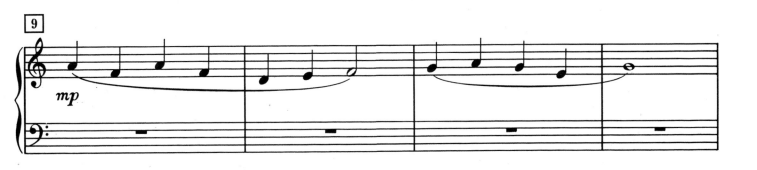

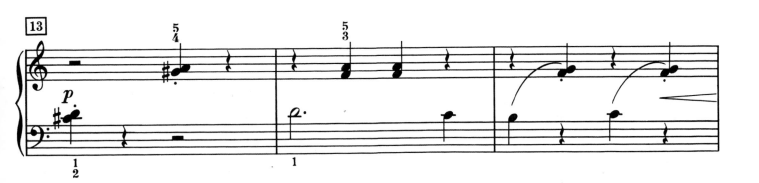

4

The Bow-Wow Chorus

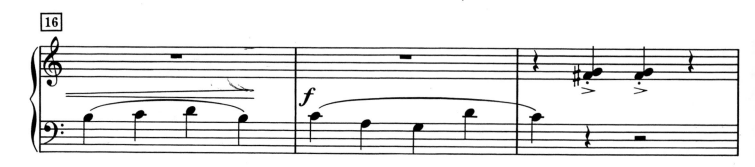

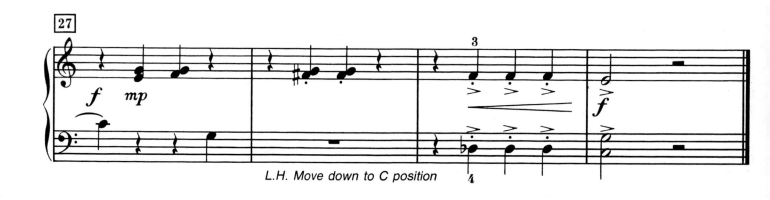

L.H. Move down to C position

The Bow-Wow Chorus

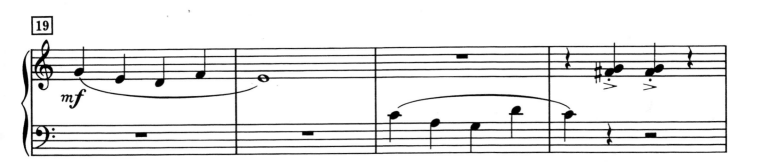

The Wagging Tail

SECONDO

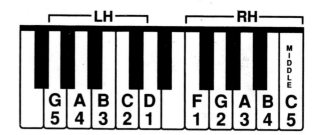

Swishing happily!

Count to primo part:

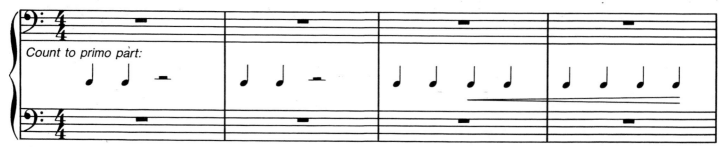

Move second finger down one step

The Wagging Tail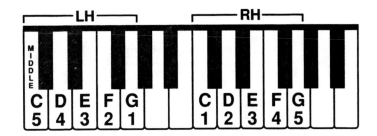*

Swishing happily!

Both hands 8va higher throughout

*The Primo part of this duet is effective as a solo.

The Wagging Tail

(*change position*)

The Wagging Tail

* If the piece is used as a solo, play the small RH letter-note in measure 20.

** Glissando is optional.

Puppy Love

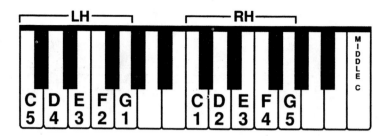

Affectionately ❤ X X X

Both hands 8va lower throughout*

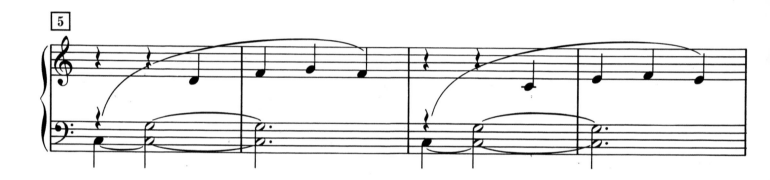

* Pedal may be used if desired (for example, measures 1-2, 3-4, etc.).
  Omit pedal in measures 32-33.

Puppy Love

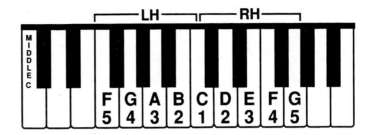

Affectionately ❤ ✗ ✗ ✗

Both hands 8va higher throughout

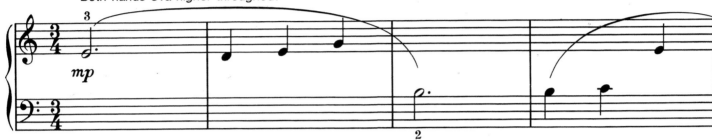

12

Puppy Love

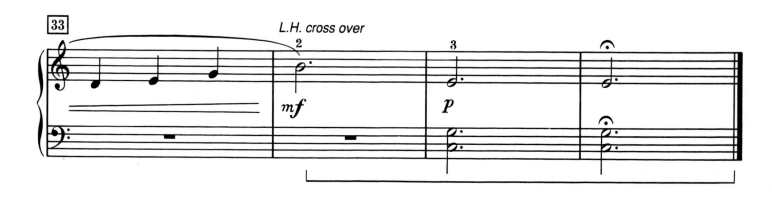

Puppy Love

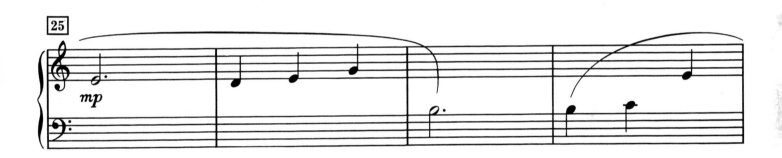

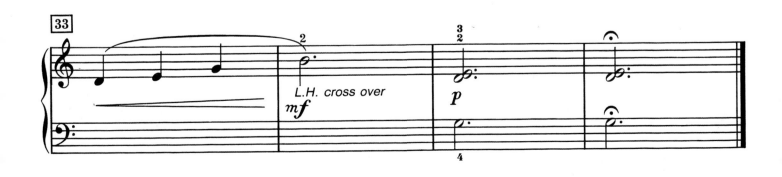

L.H. cross over

Guard Dog

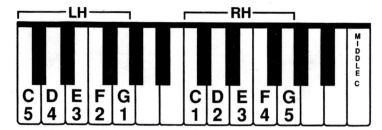

Ruff and tough

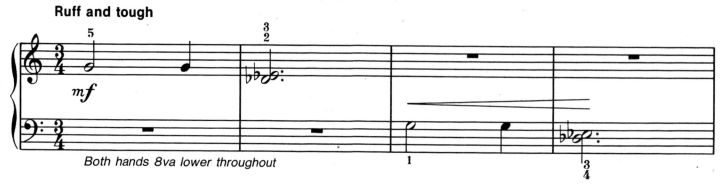

Both hands 8va lower throughout

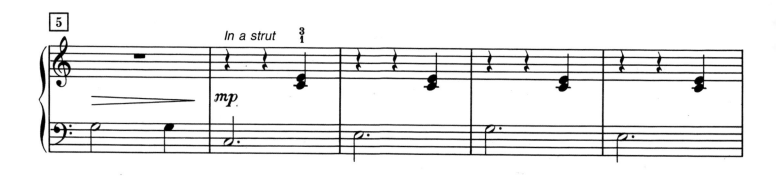

In a strut

Guard Dog

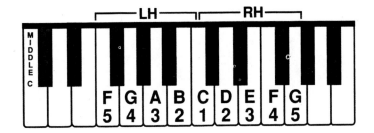

Ruff and tough

Both hands 8va higher throughout

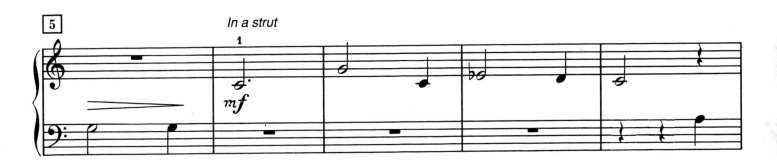

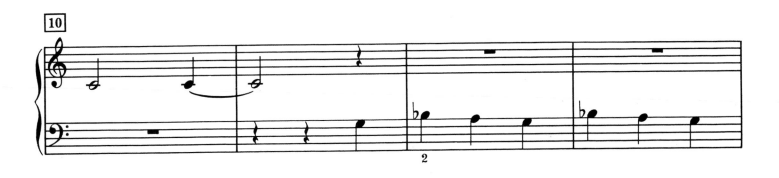

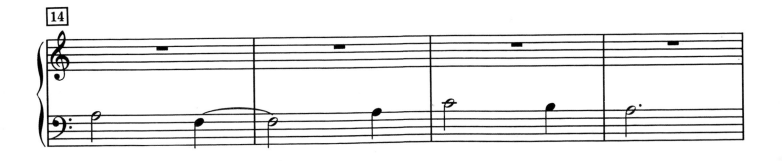

Guard Dog

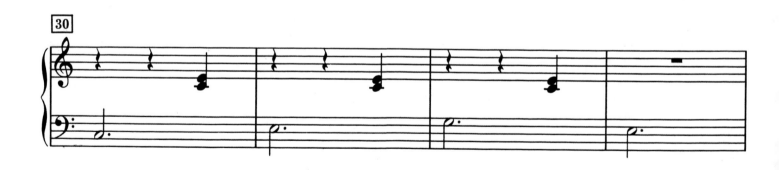

Furosciously!

Guard Dog

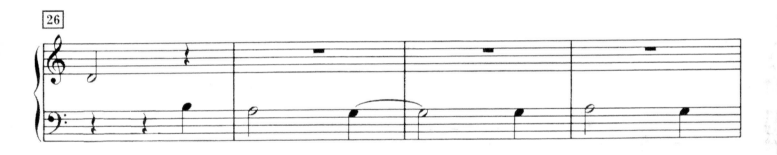

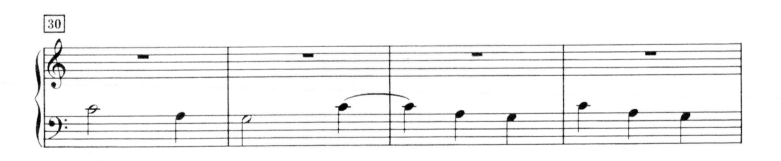

Furosciously!